Eight Things You Need to Survive

James Nugent

Disclaimer

The following is purely a general discussion. Reading this book in no way can qualify you to survive any particular crisis. It is highly recommended that you take practical survivalist training before you try to implement any of these topics. No liability is offered or accepted by this author.

Forward

From my earliest days, my father taught me to survive in multiple scenarios. He taught me to survive in three environments. They were: an aircraft crash in the mountains, a ship wreck, and being lost in the forest. In each scenario he taught me that a person needed to have seven types of tools in order to survive. Over the decades I have added an 8th type of tool. While the category of "communications" is not critical for life support, it can facilitate escape from a difficult situation. Recent advancement in technology, make communications with rescue personnel very possible.

Overview

There are eight types/categories of tools that a person needs for survival.

They are:

1. Food and Water
2. Clothing
3. Shelter
4. First Aid/ Medical Care
5. Fire
6. Rescue
7. Pioneering
8. Communications

Given these types of survival tools and the skill to use them, a person can make it out alive or even thrive for a long time.

Category One- Food and Water

You either have to carry food and water with you or harvest it on the way.

Every pint of water weighs a pound so I don't find it practical to carry more than a gallon of water total in my pack. Unless the climate is very hot and dry I usually carry only two quarts of water. I plan my route to be near natural water sources. I must carry with me a way to purify the water I encounter. I use a water filter, and way to boil water. I also carry water purification pills as a backup.

My favorite device is a straw like device which fits in a quart size drinking container. It filters and chemically treats about 500 quarts of water. I use it whenever I go into the wilderness and when I travel in the third world. I have never had a water born pathogen! As a fall back the pills will purify my drinking water if the filter malfunctions and of course boiling water is a pain but works.

Food is another difficult one. I usually carry a half a dozen granola bars. These are packed with carbohydrates and protein.

In most wilderness environments there are natural food resources. You must study to take advantage of these. You must be willing to eat most mammals and reptiles and birds. Learn to hunt and fish before you go. In most seasons there are delectable tidbits to eat.

For example some mushrooms are absolutely fabulous, but eat the wrong ones and you will die a slow painful death. Don't experiment in the field! Make harvesting wild edibles a hobby ahead of time. I don't take a manual into the woods. I learn what to eat before I get lost.

Category Two- Clothing

You must dress for the weather. Dress for heat, cold, and rain. Wear or carry rain gear. Without a waterproof shell you are subject to hypothermia. You can die.

Cotton clothes are great for heat and if dampened the can keep you cool.

Wool is still an ideal material when it is wet and cold.

You should be prepared for all three weather conditions. Special thought should be given to head gear. Protect you head from sun, cold and rain.

Category Three- Shelter

Think cocoon. If you don't have a suitable sleeping bag and tent/tarp; then you should have a plastic tube tent and a couple foil "space" thermal blankets. If you can get a good night sleep you will find it easier to survive. The few times I have unexpectedly needed to sleep out over the last 40 years; I have slept like a baby because I was prepared.

Once when and avalanched blocked the trail I figured it was better to assess the trail in good light in the morning. So I retreated to a safe place and had a very comfortable night. The next morning I had to take a mile long detour cross country to get around the slide. I only had a light day pack with me but I had everything I needed.

Another time at night, I was just 300 yards from the car and traversing a cliff. I dropped my flashlight and my headlamp went out. I could risk a fall or just kick back a rest for the night. Even when it rained, I was comfy and dry with my fanny pack survival kit. I had almost left my little kit in the car but at the last second I put it on. From this experience I learned that whenever I leave the pavement I must always have my Personal Survival Kit.

Note

Besides always carrying my 6 pound Personal Survival Kit; I always have survival kits in my car, boat or aircraft. Each kit addresses all 8 categories of survival gear.

Category Four- First Aid

Depending how remote you are going, will determine how elaborate your First Aid supplies must be. The more training you have, the better you will deal with accidents and emergencies. I spent 13 years in resident summer camps so I learned a lot first responder care. At a very minimum you should take a Red Cross First Aid and CPR class. A Wilderness First Aid Class is another good idea. If you are doing serious expedition work, talk with your Doctor about the use of prescription antibiotics, pain killers and other useful drugs.

The number one item in my first aid supplies has been a small tube of triple antibiotic ointment. I personally have never had a wound ever get infected when I have cleaned a wound and applied the ointment. I usually put a clean dressing on the wound, and keep it dry by covering it with duct tape. As long as the dressings and duct tape hold out; even my most serious injuries have been just fine.

I do not want to get other people's blood on me so I always carry a couple of plastic gloves in my supplies. There are numerous tiny commercial kits available. I have never needed to suture a wound, but I carry a suture kit on expeditions. I also carry a pint of vodka for wound cleaning on jungle trips. Infection happen rapidly in the jungle and can easily be life threatening.

Category Five- Fire

Have the ability to make a fire and boil water is critical. You will last less than 3 days without clean water. Also a well stoked fire can keep you warm and safer from animals. Learn to start and maintain a fire. It is a skill which must be practiced. The best trick I have learned is that a; wet stick, branch or log is almost always dry on the inside. Armed with this knowledge and an axe or knife you can split the wood and maintain a fire even in the rain.

Oh, but getting a fire started is another matter. I have never been able to get a fire started by rubbing two sticks together or using a bow and spindle. But I have had grand success with the following methods.

1. Matches (water proof)
2. Magnesium match
3. A 9 Volt battery and steel wool
4. Matches and vodka
5. Cotton balls soaked in Vaseline

I don't carry lighters. I think they are dangerous and twice I had them malfunction. Both times they caught on fire in my pockets. Both times I threw them and they exploded. Both times I burnt my fingers. You would think I would have learned the first time.

I also carry an aluminum cup and heavy duty foil. I can boil water in the cup and or the foil.

Practice. Practice. Practice your fire building skills.

Category Six-Rescue Equipment

You must have a way to signal for help. I carry a whistle, tiny mirror and often an Arial flare. I will not start a forest fire with the flare but in wet conditions, I want the option of attracting an aircraft. A smoky well controlled fire can draw attention too. The whistle will carry farther than voice and you won't lose your voice.

The best kind of rescue is self-rescue. Good map and compass skills are must if you want to walk out on your own. They must be practiced too. On the bright side map and compass skill add greatly to your safety and enjoyment of the outdoors. Frankly, getting lost is dangerous. Just practice every time you get a chance. You can practice even in the car.

What about GPS? Well that's good too just don't make it your only way to navigate. Trees and canopy will block GPS signals and sometimes for various reasons, GPS is just plain wrong. In my book "Night Kayaking" I recount a tale of getting turned around in the fog at night. I almost had to sleep out on a strange beach until I used a map and compass along with a GPS phone application to find my way home. Use everything available when navigating.

I have self-rescued many times. Examples would be when I was: lost in a sailboat in the San Juan Islands, lost in the Olympic Rainforest, lost in the Eastern Washington Desert, lost in a Costa Rican Jungle, and turned around at night in the Washington State Capital Forest. I have been lost so many times that one would think that I would be hesitant to leave the road. Quite the opposite, finding my way home has always been the fun part. :> After four decades; I still have never need assistance from rescue personnel.

Category Seven- Pioneering

Pioneering tools are two kinds. There are tool for constructing shelters and various structures and there are tools for defense from predators.

An axe, saw, or knife are examples of this category of tools. My favorite pioneering tool is a full Rambo style Bowie Knife. It is heavy and not socially acceptable but a great hatchet, digging tool, and hunting tool if attached to the tip of a 6' pole. Also in the handle there is a fishing kit, ring saw and a sling shot. I have experimented with using small arrows with the sling shot and it is a wicked hunting weapon.

Maybe you don't want or need a large knife but you certainly want a small pocket knife and a ring saw. Perhaps you want to lash a shelter together with parachute cord liberated from a bracelet you carry on your wrist. The important thing is to identify your needs and then get the right tool to meet the needs.

I like big knives because I can cut kindling and it makes feel better in bear country. However the night a bear came into camp and he was so close I could smell his bad breath; I shot him with two flares.

Actually the only other marauding animals I have ever encountered while camping some 1000 nights in the wilderness, is field mice and raccoons. Still I like my large knives.

Category Eight- Communications

In recent years Satellites have impacted wilderness travel. At first it was cheap GPS receivers, and then cheap satellite beacons. I use a "Spot" satellite beacon that can track my location and send preset messages. I can also send an emergency call for help if I have a clear view of the sky.

Now I can send and receive text messages via satellite and navigate by GPS enabled maps. It's all on the same handheld device! Of course, I can call for help by hitting one button and then text to my rescuers if necessary.

Basically as long as you have battery power you are connected to the outside world. I suppose that all this is good, as long as people still are self-sufficient. Nobody belongs in the woods unless they have a survival kit and a map and compass.

The Contents of my Personal Survival Kit

All this fits in a large Fanny Pack

-1 quart of water, filter straw, water pills

-6 granola bars

-Wool: hat, socks, gloves

-Plastic rain coat and pants

-tube tent, space blankets (2)

-tiny first aid kit

-waterproof matches, metal match, heavy duty foil (cooking pot) and a metal cup.

-whistle, flare, mirror

-large survival knife, and parachute cord bracelet

- hand held Satellite Communication device, map and compass

-Comfort Items: sunscreen, lip balm, bug repellent, tiny flashlights (2), reading glasses and sunglasses

This total kits weight including the water is about 6 pounds. I have gotten so used to carrying the kit that I don't even notice it. This kit contains the Mountaineer Ten Essentials.

Survival Incident

I once survived two night and three days with only this kit. I had gone on a long day hike and fallen down a 30 foot cliff. I spent the first night at the bottom of the cliff with a badly twisted ankle. Fortunately I was stuck next to a creek which had trout. I used my fishing kit from the handle of my knife to capture a nice dinner and breakfast. It took a full day to get to the top of the cliff. The second night I ate granola bars. The third day I cut some homemade crutches and hobble out. A kind couple offered to carry me out but I was relatively pain free and making steady progress. Besides I wanted to see if I could do it!

My philosophy

Human beings are very fragile when up against the natural world. We must prepare our survival skills and carry proper survival tools. If we don't we may needlessly die. If we do we can easily thrive.

Car Survival Kit

In the trunk of my car I have the same categories of survival gear but I am not as concerned about weight. For example I have canned food (tuna) and an axe and a full cook kit. I also have a come-along. This is a hand operated pulley system. It is for self-rescue. I figure if I can move my car one inch; I can eventually move it out of a ditch. I have used it when I slipped off the road in the snow.

Sailboat Survival Kit

My "go bad" is big, waterproof, and it floats. The only unusual item is a dry suit which I keep on top. I can put it on in about 60 seconds. Cold salt water is deadly. The rest of the gear is from the eight survival categories.

Aircraft Survival Kit

Because of weight restrictions, I just use my Personal Survival Kit and sometimes a 410 shotgun. I also make sure that I am wearing what I want to walk out it in. I have never crashed an airplane, but it looks really difficult to survive in the mountains.

Home Survival Kit

In my home we are prepared for winter power outages too. This happens most winters for a few days and once in a while for up to ten days.

Here is a list by category.

Food- We have two week's worth of extra no cook foods. For example: peanut butter, crackers, canned fruit/vegetables and ten gallons water.

Clothing- We locate our winter clothes before we need them.

Shelter- We have plastic blue tarps and duct tape. The tarps are for broken windows and sealing off one small room in order to keep it warmer.

First Aid – plentiful supplies for wound care and pain relief.

Fire- We have a variety of fuels and stoves and heaters. All heaters are safe to use in the house. We have a supply of candle and matches.

Rescue- We have poster paper and pens to place in our windows. We can write, "all is well or Ebola free". If we need to call for help we can set off a car alarm.

Pioneering- twine, rope, axe, saws, hunting equipment, household tools

Communications

Cell Phones, Ham radios, CB radios, Satellite Communications

Location

When I chose where I was going to live, I purposely chose a location which was supportive of survival. I live in a trailer at a saltwater beach outside of the city. In a pinch, crab and fish can be had year round. It is a rural setting yet close enough to the city to make resupply easy.

I have made friends with my neighbors who have an apple orchard. I dehydrate apple bits and store them for winter and spring eating. I harvest the blackberries and mushrooms which are plentiful. The berries go in a freezer and the mushrooms are dehydrated. Deer visit regularly and I have a hunting bow. The plan is to share the meat with the neighbors.

Basically no matter what the cause of the survival crisis, the location lends itself to long term survival. There is even a stream on the property which can be purified.

Action Vs Reaction

It is always desirable to act instead of react in a survival situation. The survival situation can be: an Ebola epidemic, an economic collapse, a power outage or being lost in the woods. If you plan ahead and have the necessary knowledge and skills; one can seamlessly continue on with life.

A Personal Reflection

I am thinking back to my twisted ankle drama. Except for the pain it was actually fun. The trout were the best baked fish I have ever eaten. I slept on a moss padded logs and by elevating my ankle all night; it was much improved in the morning. If I didn't have my Personal Survival Kit; it would have not worked so well.

Spiritual Resources

One reason I never freak out in a survival situation is my belief system. I believe in a good and loving God. While none of us get out of this world without dying; I have reason for optimism and hope in an afterlife. This plants me securely in the present and takes almost all of the stress out of coping. The time to develop spiritual resources is before there is a crisis. Just like your plant identification and fire starting skills; spiritual skills need to be practiced.

James Nugent

Olympia WA   11-13-14

Books by James Nugent

Eight Things You Need to Survive

Writing My First Books

How I Sailed From Olympia to the San Juan Islands, and Returned Safely

An Alternative Boating Guide to Southern Puget Sound

How and Why I lived Aboard

Kayaking Budd Inlet in South Puget Sound

Night Kayaking

Writing E-books and Making the Perfect Book

I Speak Esperanto

The Rainbow Road and Other Signs of God's Love

Living an Abundant Life, Within Your Means

Social Jujitsu and Powerful Principles for Managing Social Conflict

Blackjack on My Small Budget

A Little Benedictine Oblate Manuel

Without Speech

All things work

Loving Time with Your Creator

Personal Adventures in a Life of Learning

The Good News about Being Catholic

E-book Writing and Overcoming Barriers to Creativity

E-book Writing and Organizing Your Ideas

My Forty Days for Life 2013

Lifestyle Reality Observing

How to Sail in the Winter

How to Get Your Kid to Move Out

How to Get What Want

Sex, Abstinence, and Happiness

Cynthia Says Radio Show – Anger is a choice

More Good News about Being Catholic

The Solo Kayak

A Beach Naturalist on Southern Puget Sound

Clean House Clean Life

The Total Catholic Christian

Happiness is a Choice

Solo Kayak II

The Extraordinary Eucharistic Visitor

The Catholic Way of Dying

Available at Amazon.com in Kindle E-Book and or Audible Book or Paperback

www.ingramcontent.com/pod-product-compliance
Lightning Source LLC
Chambersburg PA
CBHW070754010626
R18375000001B/R183750PG45790CBX00001B/1